Contents

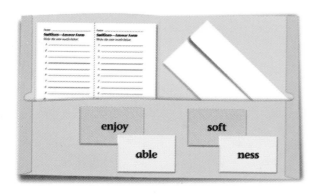

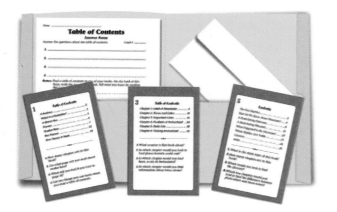

Literacy Centers 3-4

What's Great About This Book

Centers are a wonderful, fun way for students to practice important skills. The 16 centers in this book are self-contained and portable. Students may work at a desk or even on the floor. Once you've made the centers, they're ready to use at any time.

Everything You Need

- Teacher direction page includes how to make the center and a description of the student task

- Full-color materials needed for the center

- Reproducible answer forms

How to Use the Centers

The centers are intended for skill practice, not to introduce skills. It is important to model the use of each center before students do the task independently.

Questions to Consider:

- Will students select a center, or will you assign the centers?
- Will there be a specific block of time for centers, or will the centers be used throughout the day?
- Where will you place the centers for easy access by students?
- What procedure will students use when they need help with the center tasks?
- Where will students store completed work?
- How will you track the tasks and centers completed by each student?

Making a File Folder Center

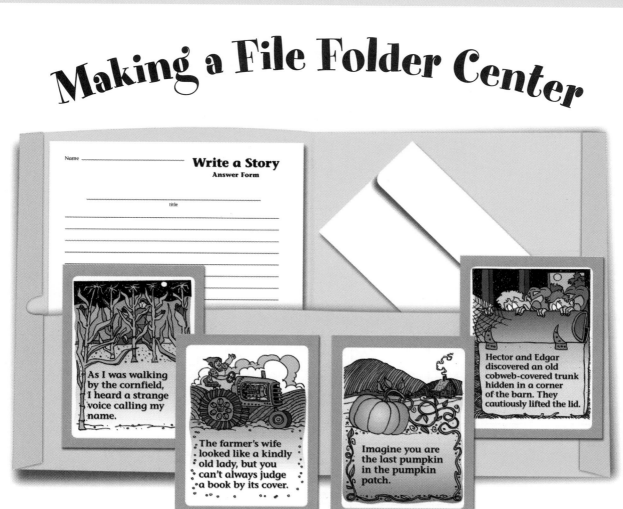

Materials

- folder with pockets
- envelopes
- marking pens
- glue
- tape

Folder centers are easily stored in a box or file crate. Students take a folder to their desks to complete the task.

Steps to Follow

1. Remove and laminate the cover design. Glue it to the front of the folder.
2. Laminate the student directions and glue it to the back of the folder.
3. Place answer forms, writing paper, and any other supplies in the left-hand pocket.
4. Place each set of task cards in an envelope in the right-hand pocket.

Center Checklist

Student Names

Centers

Analogies												
Multiple-Meaning Words												
Prefixes												
Suffixes												
Main Idea and Supporting Details												
Antonyms												
Synonyms												
Combining Sentences												
Alphabetical Order												
Writing Descriptive Paragraphs												
Similes												
Fact or Opinion?												
Parts of Speech												
Table of Contents												
Using an Index												
Write a Story												

Analogies

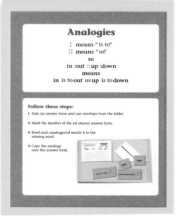

Preparing the Center

1. Prepare a folder following the directions on page 3. Laminate the cover design on page 7. Attach it to the front of the folder.

2. Laminate the student directions on page 9. Attach it to the back of the folder.

3. Laminate and cut out the task cards on pages 11, 13, and 15. Place each set in an envelope. Label the envelopes *Analogies—Set 1* (purple) and *Analogies—Set 2* (blue). Place the envelopes in the right-hand pocket of the folder.

4. Reproduce a supply of the answer form on page 6. Place copies in the left-hand pocket of the folder.

Using the Center

1. The student selects a set of task cards and marks the set number on the answer form.

2. Next, the student lays out the analogy cards and the answer cards. Then the student reads each analogy and matches it to an answer card.

3. Finally, the student copies the complete analogy onto the answer form.

Name _____

Analogies
Answer Form

Check the set of cards you are using.

Copy and complete the analogies.

Set 1 _____   Set 2 _____

Example:

eyes : _see_ :: _ears_ : _hear_

1. _____ : _____ :: _____ : _____

2. _____ : _____ :: _____ : _____

3. _____ : _____ :: _____ : _____

4. _____ : _____ :: _____ : _____

5. _____ : _____ :: _____ : _____

6. _____ : _____ :: _____ : _____

7. _____ : _____ :: _____ : _____

8. _____ : _____ :: _____ : _____

9. _____ : _____ :: _____ : _____

10. _____ : _____ :: _____ : _____

11. _____ : _____ :: _____ : _____

12. _____ : _____ :: _____ : _____

Bonus: Write and illustrate a new analogy on the back of this page.

Analogies

Analogies

: means "is to"

:: means "as"

so

in : out :: up : down

means

in is to out as up is to down

Follow these steps:

1. Take an answer form and one envelope from the folder.

2. Mark the number of the set on your answer form.

3. Read each analogy and match it to the missing word.

4. Copy the analogy onto the answer form.

Literacy Centers—Take It to Your Seat • EMC 2124

thirsty : drink :: hungry :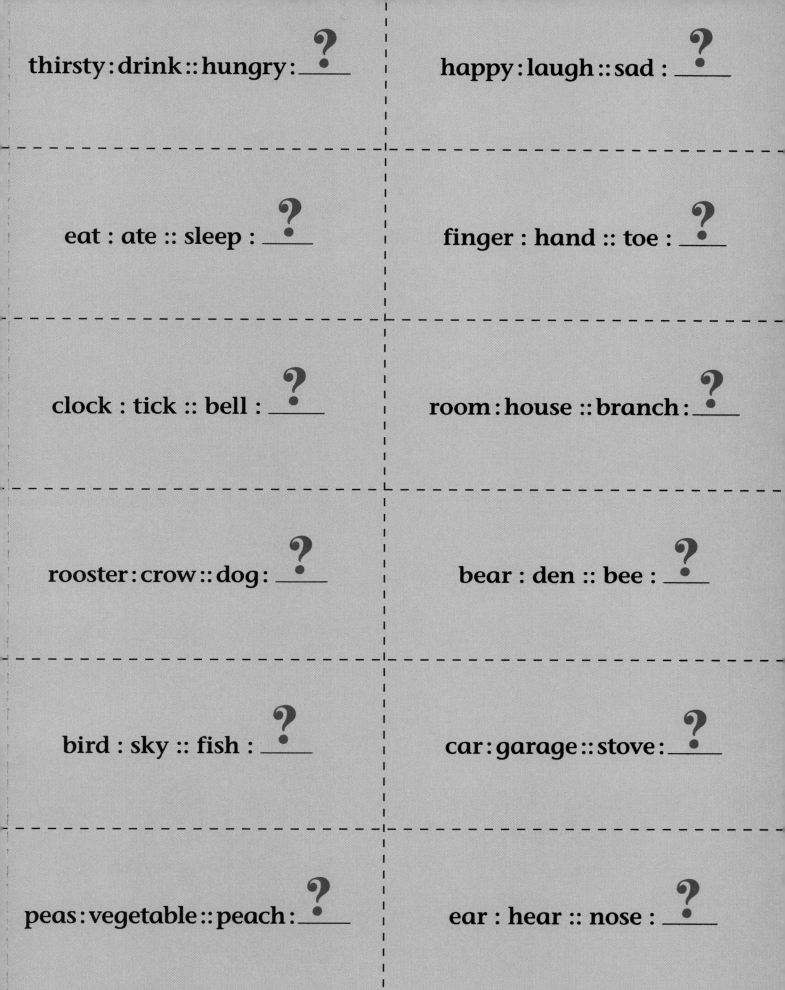

happy : laugh :: sad :

eat : ate :: sleep :

finger : hand :: toe :

clock : tick :: bell :

room : house :: branch :

rooster : crow :: dog :

bear : den :: bee :

bird : sky :: fish :

car : garage :: stove :

peas : vegetable :: peach :

ear : hear :: nose :

set

1

set

1

set

1

set

1

set

1

set

1

set

1

set

1

set

1

set

1

set

1

set

1

computer : office :: tractor : ____

paint : artist :: guitar : ____

car : driver :: plane : ____

woman : aunt :: man : ____

speedy : pokey :: heavy : ____

puppy : dog :: cub : ____

date : calendar :: time : ____

paw : bear :: fin : ____

scales : snake :: feathers : ____

hand : wrist :: foot : ____

glass : break :: paper : ____

shoes : feet :: gloves : ____

set

2

© 2003 by Evan-Moor Corp.

set

2

© 2003 by Evan-Moor Corp.

set

2

© 2003 by Evan-Moor Corp.

set

2

© 2003 by Evan-Moor Corp.

set

2

© 2003 by Evan-Moor Corp.

set

2

© 2003 by Evan-Moor Corp.

set

2

© 2003 by Evan-Moor Corp.

set

2

© 2003 by Evan-Moor Corp.

set

2

© 2003 by Evan-Moor Corp.

set

2

© 2003 by Evan-Moor Corp.

set

2

© 2003 by Evan-Moor Corp.

set

2

© 2003 by Evan-Moor Corp.

eat	cry	slept	foot
ring	tree	bark	hive
sea	kitchen	fruit	smell
farm	musician	pilot	uncle
light	bear	clock	fish
bird	ankle	tear	hands

set
1

set
1

set
1

set
1

set
1

set
1

set
1

set
1

set
1

set
1

set
1

set
1

set
2

set
2

set
2

set
2

set
2

set
2

set
2

set
2

set
2

set
2

set
2

set
2

Multiple-Meaning Words

Name _____
Write the word that completes both
sentences by the correct number.

Multiple-Meaning
Answer Form

Sentence Pair	Multiple-Meaning Word	Sentence Pair	Multiple-Meaning Word
1	_____	7	_____
2	_____	8	_____
3	_____	9	_____
4	_____	10	_____

1.
Marvin hit a home run with his new _____

The hungry _____ swooped down and
caught a fat bug.

bat

note

6.
Mother wrote a _____
explaining why I missed school. _____ to the teacher

Can you play every _____
of music? _____ in that piece

Preparing the Center

1. Prepare a folder following the directions on page 3. Laminate the cover design on page 19. Attach it to the front of the folder.

2. Laminate the student directions on page 21. Attach it to the back of the folder.

3. Laminate and cut out the task cards on pages 23, 25, 27, and 29. Place the cards in an envelope. Label the envelope *Multiple-Meaning Words*. Place the envelope in the right-hand pocket of the folder.

4. Reproduce a supply of the answer form on page 18. Place copies in the left-hand pocket of the folder.

Using the Center

1. The student reads a pair of sentences and finds the word that correctly completes both of them.

2. Then the student writes the word by the correct number on the answer form.

Multiple-Meaning
Words

A bat landed
on my head.

I hit the ball
with my bat.

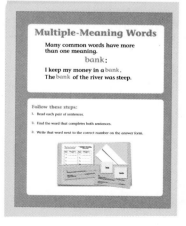

Multiple-Meaning Words

Many common words have more than one meaning.

bank:

I keep my money in a bank.
The bank of the river was steep.

Follow these steps:

1. Read each pair of sentences.

2. Find the word that completes both sentences.

3. Write that word next to the correct number on the answer form.

Name _____

Write the word that completes both
sentences by the correct number.

Multiple-Meaning Words

Answer Form

Sentence Pair	Multiple-Meaning Word	Sentence Pair	Multiple-Meaning Word
1	_____	7	_____
2	_____	8	_____
3	_____	9	_____
4	_____	10	_____
5	_____	11	_____
6	_____	12	_____

Bonus: On the back of this page, write two sentences using each of these
multiple-meaning words.

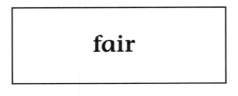

fair	mean

Multiple-Meaning Words

Literacy Centers—Take It to Your Seat • EMC 2124

Multiple-Meaning Words

Many common words have more than one meaning.

bank

I keep my money in a bank.
The bank of the river was steep.

Follow these steps:

1. Read each pair of sentences.

2. Find the word that completes both sentences.

3. Write that word next to the correct number on the answer form.

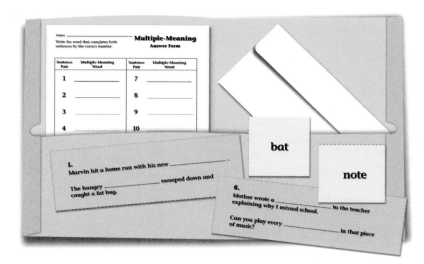

Literacy Centers—Take It to Your Seat • EMC 2124

1.

Marvin hit a home run with his new _____.

The hungry _____ swooped down and caught a fat bug.

2.

Grandfather always uses a fountain _____ to write his letters.

The frightened pig pushed open the gate and escaped from its _____.

3.

The chef poured pancake _____ onto the hot griddle.

"_____ up," called the umpire to start the baseball game.

4.

Aunt Ethel is afraid to _____ in an airplane.

A fuzzy _____ landed on my peanut butter sandwich.

5.

"I will come as fast as I _____,"
promised Mr. Lee.

Tomato soup was on sale for fifty cents a _____.

6.

Mother wrote a _____ to the teacher
explaining why I missed school.

Can you play every _____ in that piece
of music?

7.

Angela threw a dime into the wishing _____.

I was sick, but now I am feeling _____.

8.

A _____ is 36 inches long.

Father planted an orange tree in the front _____.

9.

Don't _____ over that rock. You will hurt yourself.

I've always wanted to take a _____ to the Amazon River.

10.

The stamp wouldn't _____ to the envelope.

My dog can catch a _____ no matter how far I throw it.

11.

That canoe was made from tree _____.

My dog will _____ at strangers, but he won't bite them.

12.

Toby was so excited about his birthday that he woke up as soon as it was _____ .

A bag of rocks is heavy, but a bag of feathers is _____ .

bark	bat	batter
can	fly	light
note	pen	stick
trip	well	yard

Prefixes

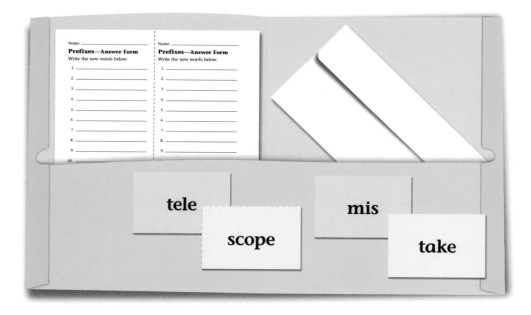

Preparing the Center

1. Prepare a folder following the directions on page 3. Laminate the cover design on page 33. Attach it to the front of the folder.

2. Laminate the student directions on page 35. Attach it to the back of the folder.

3. Laminate and cut out the task cards on pages 37 and 39. Place the cards in an envelope. Label the envelope *Prefixes*. Place the envelope in the right-hand pocket of the folder.

4. Reproduce a supply of the answer form on page 32. Place copies in the left-hand pocket of the folder.

Using the Center

1. The student matches the orange prefix cards with the yellow base word cards.

2. Then the student writes the new words on the answer form.

Name _____

Prefixes—Answer Form

Write the new words below.

1. _____
2. _____
3. _____
4. _____
5. _____
6. _____
7. _____
8. _____
9. _____
10. _____
11. _____
12. _____
13. _____
14. _____
15. _____
16. _____
17. _____
18. _____

Bonus: Choose 5 of the new words. Use each word in a sentence to show its new meaning. Write the sentences on the back of this form.

Name _____

Prefixes—Answer Form

Write the new words below.

1. _____
2. _____
3. _____
4. _____
5. _____
6. _____
7. _____
8. _____
9. _____
10. _____
11. _____
12. _____
13. _____
14. _____
15. _____
16. _____
17. _____
18. _____

Bonus: Choose 5 of the new words. Use each word in a sentence to show its new meaning. Write the sentences on the back of this form.

Prefixes

Prefixes

You will use these prefixes to make new words:

dis—not, opposite

micro—small

mis—wrong, not

tele—distant

re—again

un—not

Follow these steps:

1. Choose a yellow card. Match it to an orange prefix card to make a new word.

2. Continue to match yellow cards with orange prefix cards until you have made all 18 new words.

3. Write each new word on the answer form.

Literacy Centers—Take It to Your Seat • EMC 2124

dis	dis	dis
tele	tele	tele
micro	micro	micro
mis	mis	mis
re	re	re
un	un	un

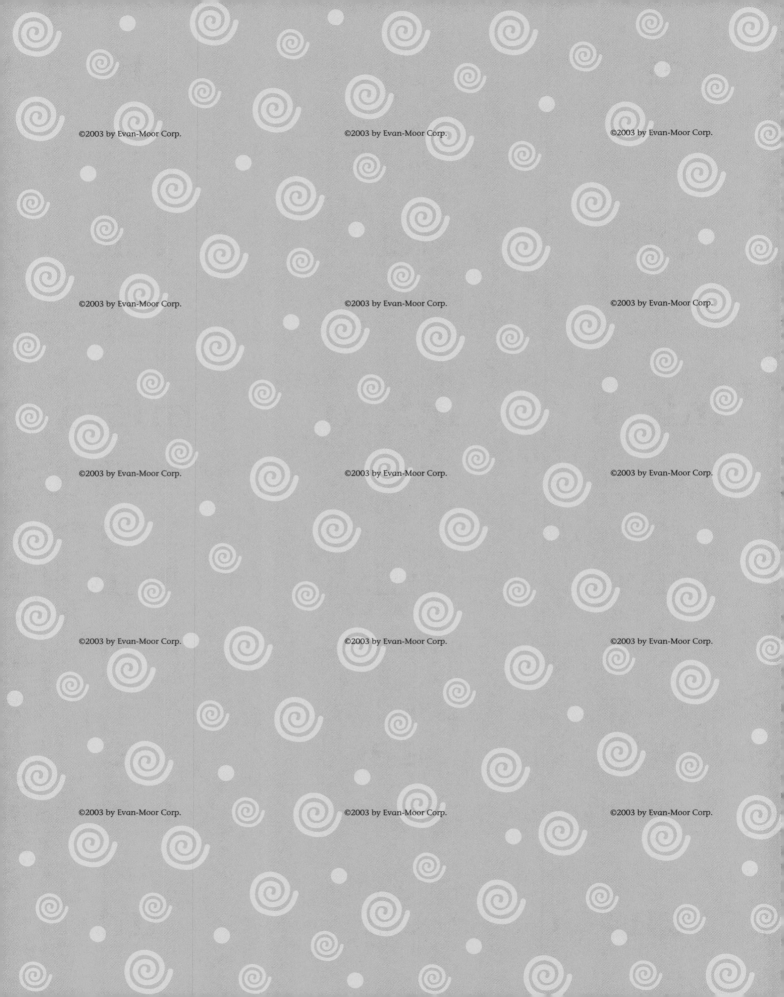

appear	agree	honest
wave	scope	phone
behave	fortune	take
phone	scope	vision
write	appear	do
comfortable	happy	able

Suffixes

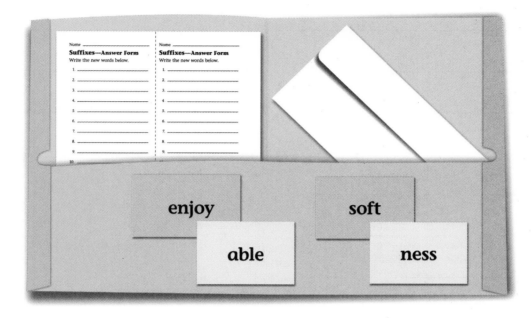

Preparing the Center

1. Prepare a folder following the directions on page 3. Laminate the cover design on page 43. Attach it to the front of the folder.

2. Laminate the student directions on page 45. Attach it to the back of the folder.

3. Laminate and cut out the task cards on pages 47 and 49. Place the cards in an envelope. Label the envelope *Suffixes*. Place the envelope in the right-hand pocket of the folder.

4. Reproduce a supply of the answer form on page 42. Place copies in the left-hand pocket of the folder.

Using the Center

1. The student matches the blue base word cards with the yellow suffix cards.

2. Then the student writes the new words on the answer form.

Suffixes—Answer Form

Write the new words below.

1. _____
2. _____
3. _____
4. _____
5. _____
6. _____
7. _____
8. _____
9. _____
10. _____
11. _____
12. _____
13. _____
14. _____
15. _____
16. _____
17. _____
18. _____

Bonus: Choose 5 of the new words. Use each word in a sentence to show its new meaning. Write the sentences on the back of this form.

Name _____

Suffixes—Answer Form

Write the new words below.

1. _____
2. _____
3. _____
4. _____
5. _____
6. _____
7. _____
8. _____
9. _____
10. _____
11. _____
12. _____
13. _____
14. _____
15. _____
16. _____
17. _____
18. _____

Bonus: Choose 5 of the new words. Use each word in a sentence to show its new meaning. Write the sentences on the back of this form.

Suffixes

Suffixes

You will use these suffixes to make new words:

ful—full of	hope**ful**
est—most	lucki**est**
er—one who	shipp**er**
ness—state or quality	happi**ness**
able—is, can be	dur**able**
en—to make	weak**en**

Follow these steps:

1. Choose a blue card. Match it to a yellow suffix card to make a new word.

2. Continue to match blue cards with yellow suffix cards until you have made all 18 new words.

3. Write each new word on the answer form.

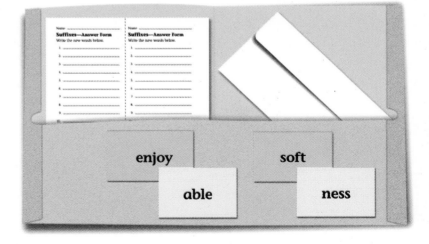

Literacy Centers—Take It to Your Seat • EMC 2124

enjoy	grace	thought
kind	sad	dark
teach	paint	dance
smart	soft	quick
comfort	perish	peace
strength	fright	length

able	able	able
er	er	er
ful	ful	ful
ness	ness	ness
en	en	en
est	est	est

Main Idea & Supporting Details

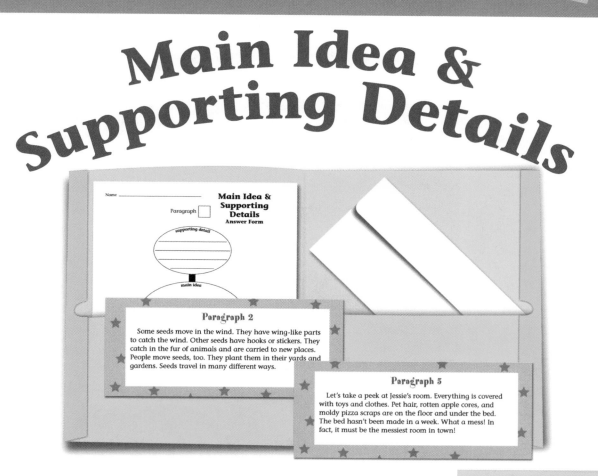

Preparing the Center

1. Prepare a folder following the directions on page 3. Laminate the cover design on page 53. Attach it to the front of the folder.

2. Laminate the student directions on page 55. Attach it to the back of the folder.

3. Laminate and cut out the task cards on pages 57 and 59. Place the cards in an envelope. Label the envelope *Main Idea & Supporting Details*. Place the envelope in the right-hand pocket of the folder.

4. Reproduce a supply of the answer form on page 52. Place copies in the left-hand pocket of the folder.

Using the Center

1. The student chooses a task card and reads the paragraph on the card.

2. Next, the student writes the main idea of the paragraph in the center of the web on the answer form.

3. Finally, the student lists the supporting details on the remaining lines of the web.

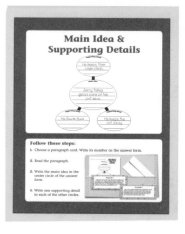

Name _____

Main Idea & Supporting Details
Answer Form

Paragraph ☐

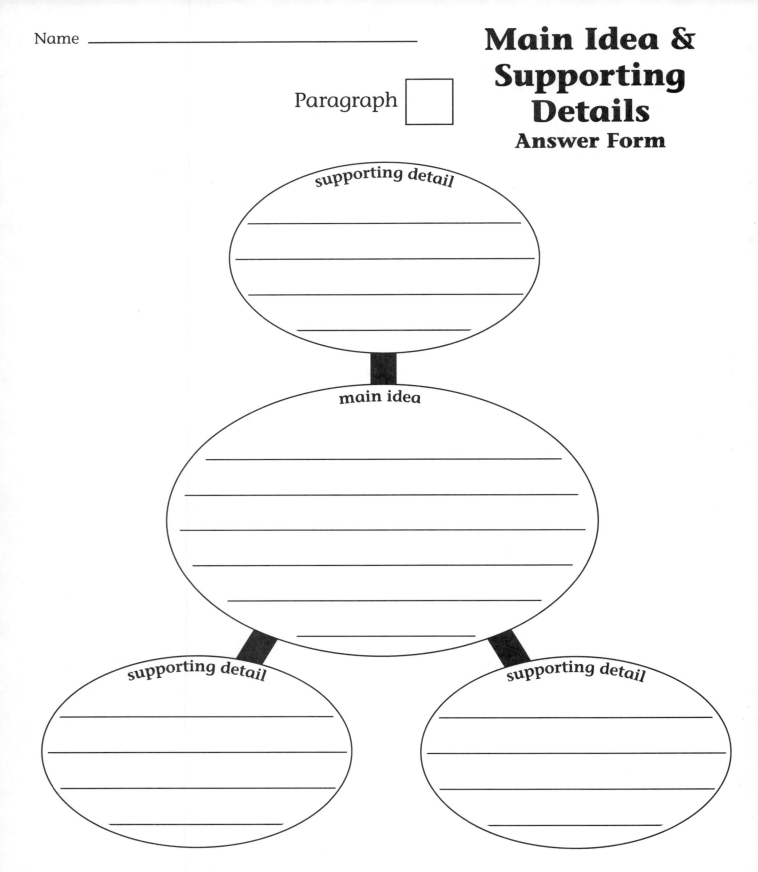

supporting detail
_____
_____
_____

main idea
_____
_____
_____
_____

supporting detail
_____
_____
_____

supporting detail
_____
_____
_____

Bonus: On the back of this page, write a paragraph about your favorite food. Underline the main idea in red and circle each supporting detail in blue.

Main Idea & Supporting Details

Main Idea & Supporting Details

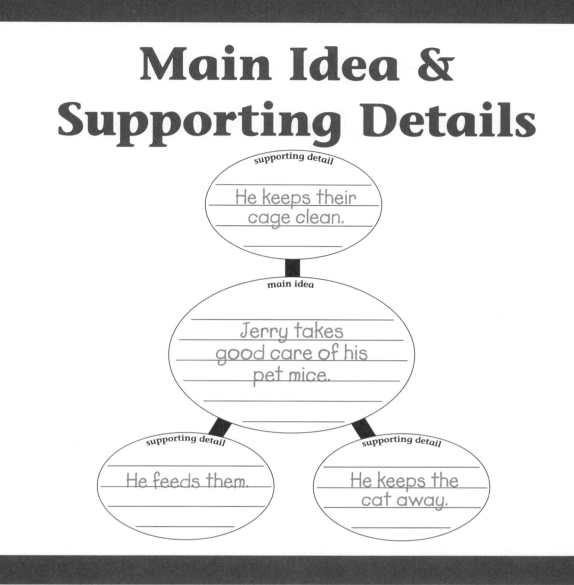

supporting detail

He keeps their cage clean.

main idea

Jerry takes good care of his pet mice.

supporting detail

He feeds them.

supporting detail

He keeps the cat away.

Follow these steps:

1. Choose a paragraph card. Write its number on the answer form.

2. Read the paragraph.

3. Write the main idea in the center circle of the answer form.

4. Write one supporting detail in each of the other circles.

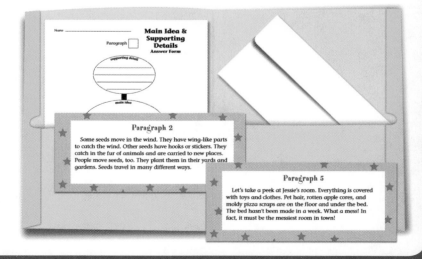

Literacy Centers—Take It to Your Seat • EMC 2124

Paragraph 1

Tonya's pet dog Brownie is very smart. Brownie can catch a Frisbee no matter how hard Tonya throws it. He can fetch the newspaper and carry it to Father. He turns a backward flip on command. Tonya thinks Brownie is the smartest pet any girl could have.

Paragraph 2

Some seeds move in the wind. They have wing-like parts to catch the wind. Other seeds have hooks or stickers. They catch in the fur of animals and are carried to new places. People move seeds, too. They plant them in their yards and gardens. Seeds travel in many different ways.

Paragraph 3

Snorkeling is a great adventure, but there are things to learn before you begin. You can learn these by taking a snorkeling class. You will learn how to breathe with a snorkel. You will learn how to dive and swim wearing a mask and fins. You will learn safety tips. Then the adventure can begin!

Paragraph 4

Karla's little brother can be a big pest. For example, yesterday he knocked over the science project Karla had been working on all week. While Karla was at school, he let her hamster out of its cage. She finally found it in her sock drawer. Then at dinner he knocked a glass of grape juice over, and the purple liquid landed in Karla's lap.

Paragraph 5

Let's take a peek at Jessie's room. Everything is covered with toys and clothes. Pet hair, rotten apple cores, and moldy pizza scraps are on the floor and under the bed. The bed hasn't been made in a week. What a mess! In fact, it must be the messiest room in town!

Paragraph 6

Did you know that a centipede is a great hunter? It stalks its prey in dark places beneath stones, logs, and piles of leaves. Then it poisons the prey with a quick bite. It catches silverfish, cockroaches, worms, and slugs.

Antonyms

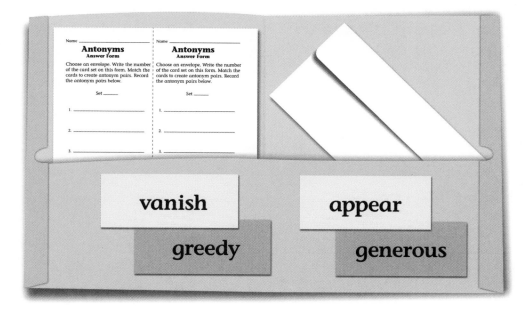

Preparing the Center

1. Prepare a folder following the directions on page 3. Laminate the cover design on page 63. Attach it to the front of the folder.

2. Laminate the student directions on page 65. Attach it to the back of the folder.

3. Laminate and cut out the task cards on pages 67 and 69. Place each set of cards in an envelope. Label the envelopes *Antonyms—Set 1* and *Antonyms—Set 2*. Place the envelopes in the right-hand pocket of the folder.

4. Reproduce a supply of the answer form on page 62. Place copies in the left-hand pocket of the folder.

Using the Center

1. The student selects a set of cards and writes the number of the card set on the answer form.

2. Next, the student matches the task cards to create antonym pairs.

3. Finally, the student records the antonyms.

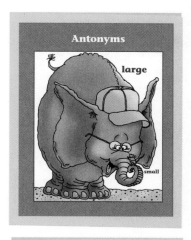

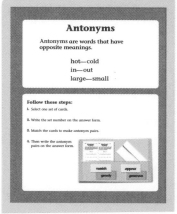

Name _____

Antonyms
Answer Form

Choose an envelope. Write the number of the card set below. Match the cards to create antonym pairs. Record the antonym pairs below.

Set _____

1. _____

2. _____

3. _____

4. _____

5. _____

6. _____

Bonus: Choose three antonym pairs and write sentences on the back of this form.

Name _____

Antonyms
Answer Form

Choose an envelope. Write the number of the card set below. Match the cards to create antonym pairs. Record the antonym pairs below.

Set _____

1. _____

2. _____

3. _____

4. _____

5. _____

6. _____

Bonus: Choose three antonym pairs and write sentences on the back of this form.

Antonyms

large

small

Antonyms

Antonyms are words that have opposite meanings.

hot—cold

in—out

large—small

Follow these steps:

1. Select one set of cards.

2. Write the set number on the answer form.

3. Match the cards to make antonym pairs.

4. Then write the antonym pairs on the answer form.

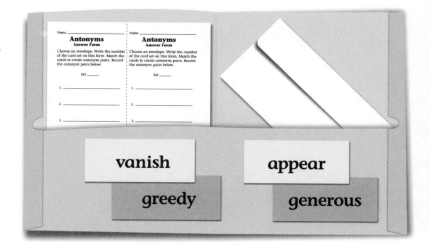

Literacy Centers—Take It to Your Seat • EMC 2124

dawn	sunset
answer	question
follow	lead
greedy	generous
innocent	guilty
liquid	solid

set

1

set

1

set

1

set

1

set

1

set

1

set

1

set

1

set

1

set

1

set

1

set

1

create	destroy
problem	solution
vanish	appear
loose	tight
timid	bold
unique	common

set

2

set

2

set

2

set

2

set

2

set

2

set

2

set

2

set

2

set

2

set

2

set

2

Synonyms

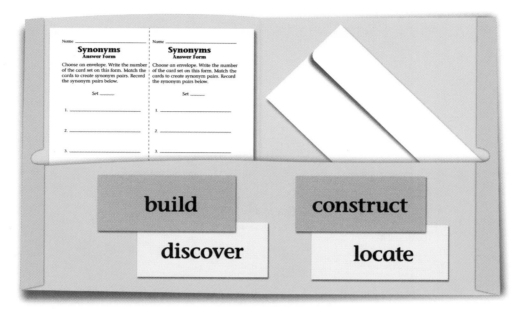

Preparing the Center

1. Prepare a folder following the directions on page 3. Laminate and cut out the cover design on page 73. Attach it to the front of the folder.

2. Laminate the student directions on page 75. Attach it to the back of the folder.

3. Laminate and cut out the task cards on pages 77 and 79. Place each set of cards in an envelope. Label the envelopes *Synonyms—Set 1* and *Synonyms—Set 2*. Place the envelopes in the right-hand pocket of the folder.

4. Reproduce a supply of the answer form on page 72. Place copies in the left-hand pocket of the folder.

Using the Center

1. The student selects a set of cards and writes the number of the card set on the answer form.

2. Next, the student matches the task cards to create synonym pairs.

3. Finally, the student records the synonyms.

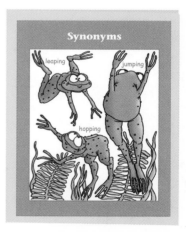

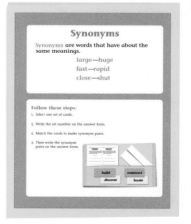

Name _____

Synonyms
Answer Form

Choose an envelope. Write the number of the card set below. Match the cards to create synonym pairs. Record the synonym pairs below.

Set _____

1. _____

2. _____

3. _____

4. _____

5. _____

6. _____

Bonus: Choose three synonym pairs and write sentences on the back of this form.

Name _____

Synonyms
Answer Form

Choose an envelope. Write the number of the card set below. Match the cards to create synonym pairs. Record the synonym pairs below.

Set _____

1. _____

2. _____

3. _____

4. _____

5. _____

6. _____

Bonus: Choose three synonym pairs and write sentences on the back of this form.

Synonyms

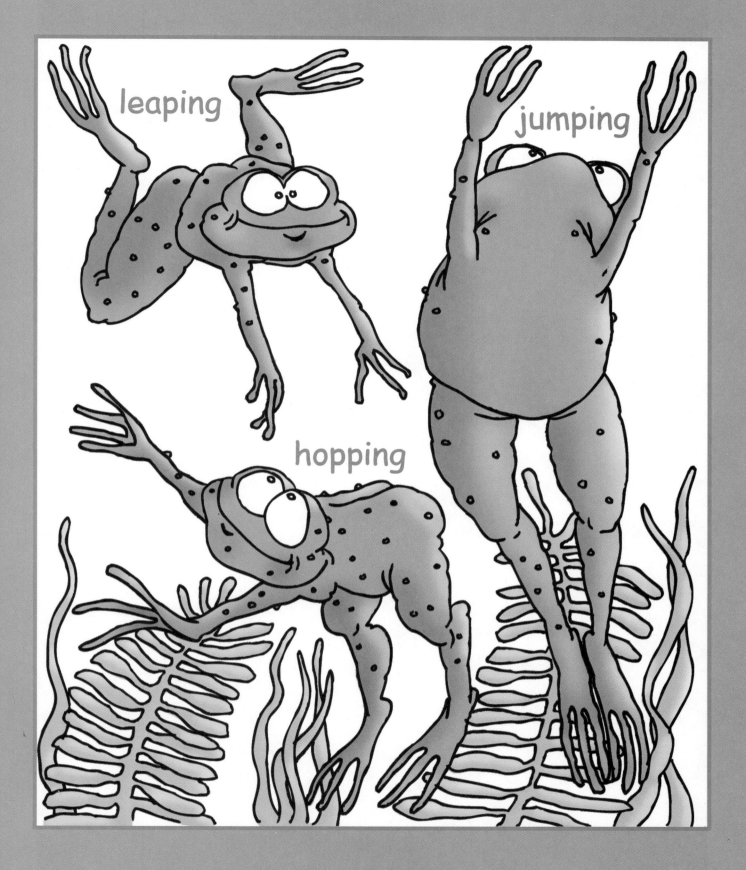

Synonyms

Synonyms are words that have about the same meaning.

large—huge

fast—rapid

close—shut

Follow these steps:

1. Select one set of cards.

2. Write the set number on the answer form.

3. Match the cards to make synonym pairs.

4. Then write the synonym pairs on the answer form.

build   construct

discover   locate

76

story	tale
grab	seize
build	construct
mistake	error
mend	repair
use	operate

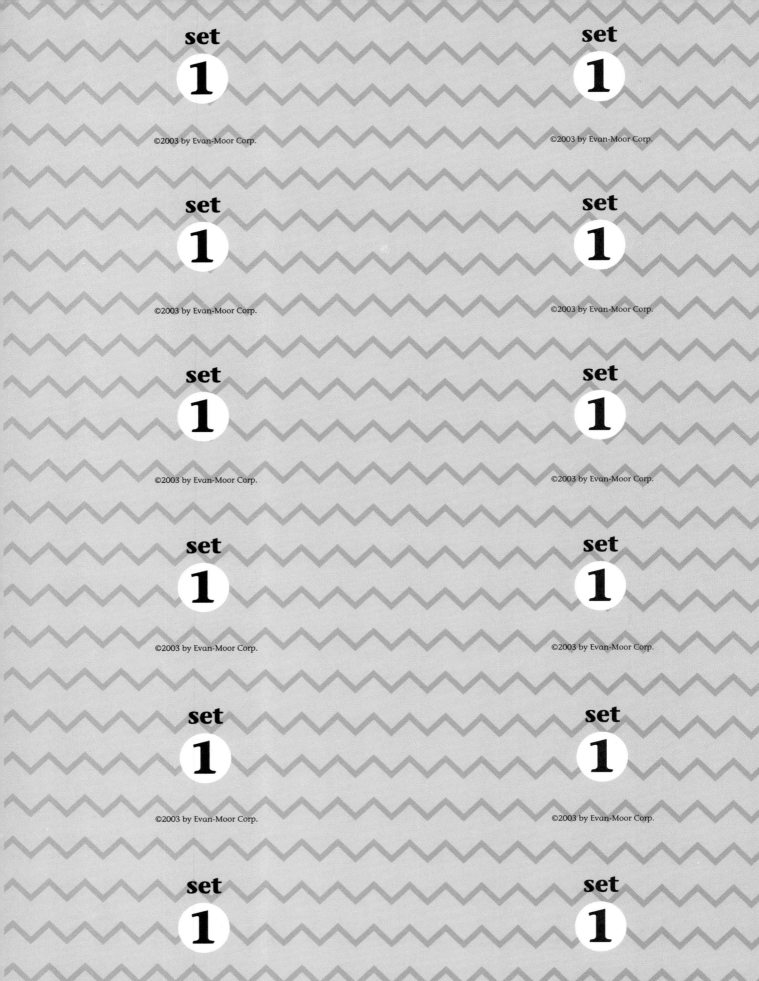

set

1

set

1

set

1

set

1

set

1

set

1

set

1

set

1

set

1

set

1

set

1

set

1

answer	reply
locate	discover
divide	separate
eat	consume
grateful	thankful
freedom	liberty

set

2

Combining Sentences

Name _____

Write the card number on the answer form. Combine the two sentences into one sentence. Write the sentences below.

Combining Sentences
Answer Form

Card Number ☐ _____
Card Number ☐ _____
Card Number ☐ _____
Card Number ☐ _____
Card

2.
Bob learned to do a cartwheel.
He learned to do a back flip, too.

6.
Cleaning my room is hard work.
My mom always gives me a snack when I finish.

Preparing the Center

1. Prepare a folder following the directions on page 3. Laminate the cover design on page 83. Attach it to the front of the folder.

2. Laminate the student directions on page 85. Attach it to the back of the folder.

3. Laminate and cut out the task cards on pages 87, 89, 91, and 93. Place the cards in an envelope. Label the envelope *Combining Sentences*. Place the envelope in the right-hand pocket of the folder.

4. Reproduce a supply of the answer form on page 82. Place copies in the left-hand pocket of the folder.

Using the Center

1. The student chooses a task card and reads the two related sentences on the card.

2. Then the student combines the sentences into a single sentence and writes the sentence on the answer form.

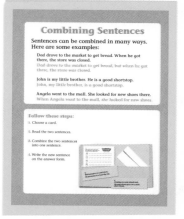

Name _____

Write the card number in the box.
Combine the two sentences into one
sentence. Write the new sentence below.

Combining Sentences

Answer Form

Card
Number

☐ _____
_____

Card
Number

☐ _____
_____

Card
Number

☐ _____
_____

Card
Number

☐ _____
_____

Card
Number

☐ _____
_____

Card
Number

☐ _____
_____

Card
Number

☐ _____
_____

Card
Number

☐ _____
_____

Bonus: Underline in red each sentence where you used a connecting word
such as **and**, **to**, **but**, **since**, or **because**.

Combining Sentences

Combining Sentences

Sentences can be combined in many ways. Here are some examples:

Dad drove to the market to get bread. When he got there, the store was closed.

Dad drove to the market to get bread, but when he got there, the store was closed.

John is my little brother. He is a good shortstop.

John, my little brother, is a good shortstop.

Angela went to the mall. She looked for new shoes there.

When Angela went to the mall, she looked for new shoes.

Follow these steps:

1. Choose a card.

2. Read the two sentences.

3. Combine the two sentences into one sentence.

4. Write the new sentence on the answer form.

1.

Jean went to a lake in the mountains.

She wanted to go hiking.

2.

Bob learned to do a cartwheel.

He learned to do a back flip, too.

3.

Mom drove to the gas station to get gas.

When she got there, the gas station was closed.

4.

Jerome got a bike for his birthday.

He got a new helmet, too.

5.

Tom's umbrella broke when the wind blew.

He got soaked.

6.

Cleaning my room is hard work.

My mom always gives me a snack when I finish.

7.

The florist brought flowers.

It's my mother's birthday today.

8.

Aunt Hazel made a dress for me.

She made a shirt for my brother Sam.

9.

Whiskers is a frisky dog.

He likes to chase the cat.

10.

Amos and Henry are my friends.

We like to swim in the pool.

11.

Mrs. Carter is my coach.

She taught me how to kick the soccer ball hard.

12.

Carlos is my cousin.

He is a good artist.

13.

Mr. Chin is my teacher.

He always helps me when I have
a question.

14.

Kris fell off his scooter.

He learned that motor scooters can be
dangerous.

15.

There was a storm last night.

This morning, there were puddles
everywhere.

16.

The autumn leaves turn color.

Squirrels begin to store nuts for the winter.

Alphabetical Order

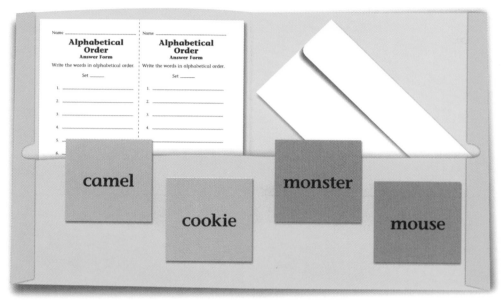

Preparing the Center

1. Prepare a folder following the directions on page 3. Laminate the cover design on page 97. Attach it to the front of the folder.

2. Laminate the student directions on page 99. Attach it to the back of the folder.

3. Laminate and cut out the task cards on pages 101, 103, and 105. Place each set of cards in an envelope. Label the envelopes *Alphabetical Order—Set 1*, *Alphabetical Order—Set 2*, and *Alphabetical Order—Set 3*. Place the envelopes in the right-hand pocket of the folder.

4. Reproduce a supply of the answer form on page 96. Place copies in the left-hand pocket of the folder.

Using the Center

1. The student selects one set of cards and writes the number of the set on the answer form.

2. Next, the student places the cards in alphabetical order.

3. Finally, the student copies the words in alphabetical order onto the answer form.

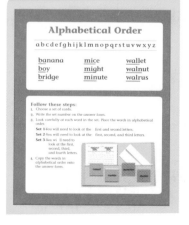

Name _____

Alphabetical Order

Answer Form

Write the words in alphabetical order.

Set _____

1. _____

2. _____

3. _____

4. _____

5. _____

6. _____

7. _____

8. _____

9. _____

10. _____

11. _____

12. _____

Bonus: Write the names of 10 people you know in alphabetical order on the back of this form.

Name _____

Alphabetical Order

Answer Form

Write the words in alphabetical order.

Set _____

1. _____

2. _____

3. _____

4. _____

5. _____

6. _____

7. _____

8. _____

9. _____

10. _____

11. _____

12. _____

Bonus: Write the names of 10 people you know in alphabetical order on the back of this form.

Alphabetical Order

Alphabetical Order

a b c d e f g h i j k l m n o p q r s t u v w x y z

banana
boy
bridge

mice
might
minute

wallet
walnut
walrus

Follow these steps:

1. Choose a set of cards.
2. Write the set number on the answer form.
3. Look carefully at each word in the set. Place the words in alphabetical order.

   Set 1—You will need to look at the first and second letters.

   Set 2—You will need to look at the first, second, and third letters.

   Set 3—You will need to look at the first, second, third, and fourth letters.

4. Copy the words in alphabetical order onto the answer form.

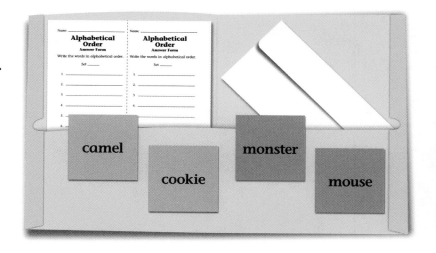

Litteracy Centers—Take It to Your Seat • EMC 2124

camel	cookie	city
gauze	ground	glance
tiny	thunder	trailer
pickle	peculiar	phone

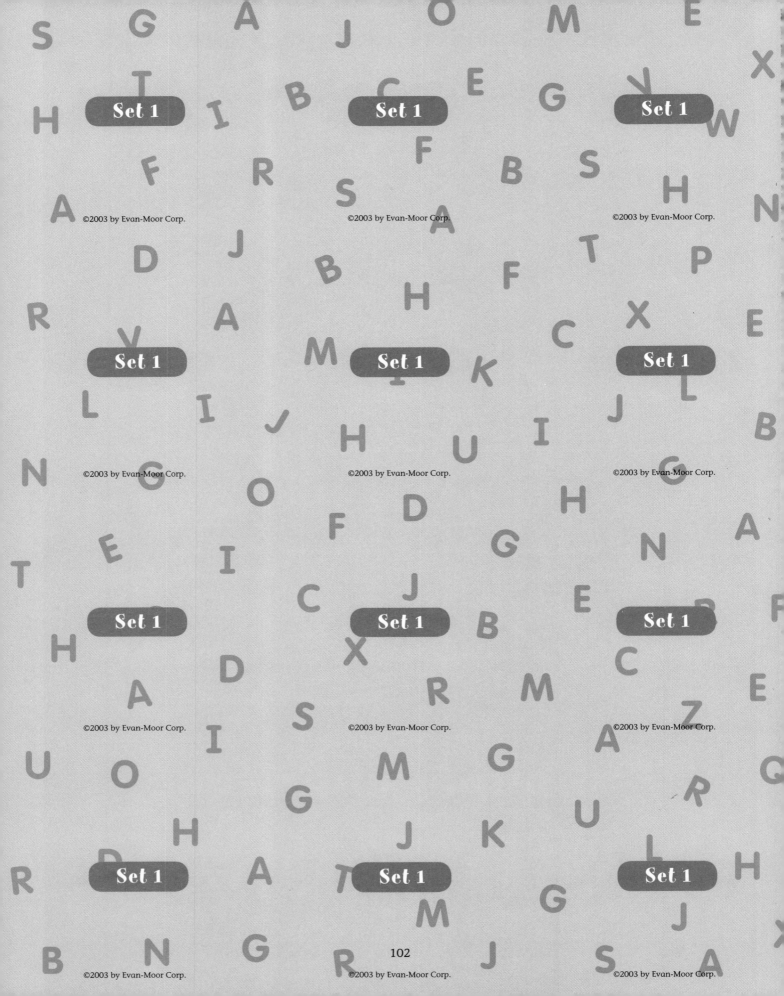

Set 1

Set 1

Set 1

Set 1

Set 1

Set 1

Set 1

Set 1

Set 1

Set 1

Set 1

Set 1

racket	rattle	rake
raisin	money	motel
monster	mouse	fast
fantasy	faint	family

Set 2

Set 2

Set 2

Set 2

Set 2

Set 2

Set 2

Set 2

Set 2

Set 2

Set 2

Set 2

barge	barn	bargain
bark	weather	weave
wear	weapon	grace
grammar	grape	graph

Set 3

Set 3

Set 3

Set 3

Set 3

Set 3

Set 3

Set 3

Set 3

Set 3

Set 3

Set 3

Writing Descriptive Paragraphs

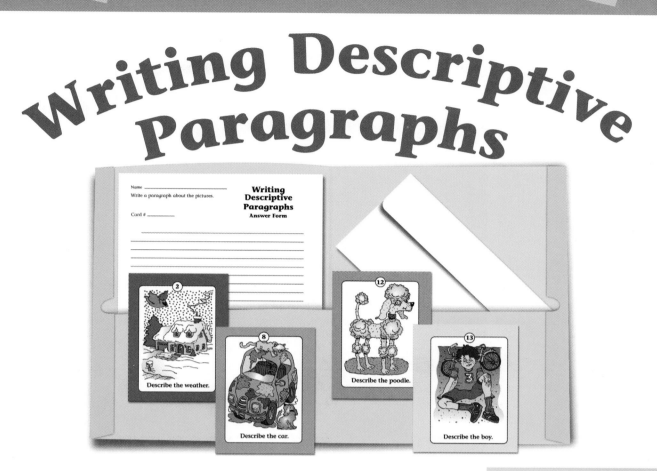

Preparing the Center

1. Prepare a folder following the directions on page 3. Laminate the cover design on page 109. Attach it to the front of the folder.

2. Laminate the student directions on page 111. Attach it to the back of the folder.

3. Laminate and cut out the task cards on pages 113, 115, 117, and 119. Place the cards in an envelope. Label the envelope *Write Descriptive Paragraphs*. Place the envelope in the right-hand pocket of the folder.

4. Reproduce a supply of the answer form on page 108. Place copies in the left-hand pocket of the folder.

Using the Center

1. The student selects a picture card and writes the card number on the answer form.

2. Next, the student reads the directions on the card.

3. Finally, the student writes a descriptive paragraph about the picture on the answer form.

Name _____

Card # _____

Writing Descriptive Paragraphs
Answer Form

Write a paragraph about the picture.

_____

_____

_____

_____

_____

_____

_____

_____

_____

_____

_____

_____

_____

_____

_____

Bonus: On the back of this page, list the descriptive words you used in your
paragraph.

Writing Descriptive Paragraphs

Writing Descriptive Paragraphs

A descriptive paragraph helps make a picture of a character, place, or event in the reader's mind.

Follow these steps:

1. Choose a picture card, write the card number on the answer form, and read the direction sentence.

   Describe the wagon.

2. Think about adjectives that you might use to describe the picture.

   old   rusty   crooked wheel   broken handle

3. Imagine how your five senses could help in describing the picture.

   hear a creaking noise   a moldy smell   wood feels rough

4. Write your paragraph.

   This old, rusty wagon belonged to my grandfather when he was a boy. It was shiny and new then. Now the wooden sides are rough and full of splinters. The old wagon smells moldy like old leaves under a tree. When I pull on the broken handle, the crooked wheels creak and the sides rattle.

Describe how he feels.

Describe the weather.

Describe the sundae.

Describe the elephant.

5

Describe how she feels.

6

Describe the weather.

7

Describe the pet hamster

8

Describe the car.

9

Describe the flag.

10

Describe the weather.

11

Describe the pizza.

12

Describe the poodle.

13 Describe the boy.

14 Describe the lady.

15 Describe the bouquet.

16 Describe the campfire.

Similles

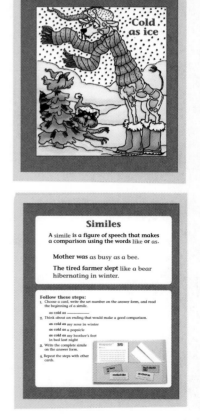

Preparing the Center

1. Prepare a folder following the directions on page 3. Laminate the cover design on page 123. Attach it to the front of the folder.

2. Laminate the student directions on page 125. Attach it to the back of the folder.

3. Laminate and cut out the task cards on pages 127 and 129. Place the cards in envelopes labeled *Similes—Set 1* and *Similes—Set 2*. Place the envelopes in the right-hand pocket of the folder.

4. Reproduce a supply of the answer form on page 122. Place copies in the left-hand pocket of the folder.

Using the Center

1. The student selects a card and writes the set number on the answer form.

2. Next, the student reads the simile and thinks of a word that completes it.

3. Finally, the student copies the simile and adds a word or words to complete it on the answer form.

Name _____

Set _____

Write the complete simile below.

1. _____

2. _____

3. _____

4. _____

5. _____

6. _____

7. _____

8. _____

9. _____

10. _____

11. _____

12. _____

Bonus: Make up five new similes. Write them on the back of this page.

Similes

Cold as ice

Similes

A **simile** is a figure of speech that makes a comparison using the words **like** or **as**.

Mother was as busy as a bee.

The tired farmer slept like a bear hibernating in winter.

Follow these steps:

1. Choose a card, write the set number on the answer form, and read the beginning of a simile.

   as cold as _____

2. Think about an ending that would make a good comparison.

   as cold as my nose in winter

   as cold as a popsicle

   as cold as my brother's feet in bed last night

3. Write the complete simile on the answer form.

4. Repeat the steps with other cards.

as busy as _____	as bright as _____
waddled like _____	as flat as _____
as sly as _____	had cheeks like _____
as strong as _____	as light as _____
chattered like _____	fought like _____
as smart as _____	as cute as _____

set

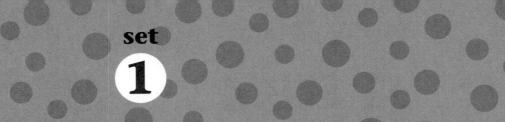

1

set

1

set

1

set

1

set

1

set

1

set

1

set

1

set

1

set

1

set

1

set

1

as stubborn as _____	as slow as _____
worked like _____	as hungry as _____
slept like _____	as smooth as _____
as comfortable as _____	as cold as _____
laughed like _____	as clear as _____
as hard as _____	sparkled like _____

set

2

set

2

set

2

set

2

set

2

set

2

set

2

set

2

set

2

set

2

Fact or Opinion?

Name _____
Read each sentence. Decide if it states a fact or an opinion. Write the sentence number in the correct box.

Fact or Opinion?
Answer Form

Fact	Opinion

1 A cat is the best kind of pet.

11 Everyone likes funny movies.

8 It is good to brush your teeth after every meal.

12 Playing with matches is dangerous.

Preparing the Center

1. Prepare a folder following the directions on page 3. Laminate the cover design on page 133. Attach it to the front of the folder.

2. Laminate the student directions on page 135. Attach it to the back of the folder.

3. Laminate and cut out the task cards on pages 137 and 139. Place the cards in an envelope. Label the envelope *Fact or Opinion?* Place the envelope in the right-hand pocket of the folder.

4. Reproduce a supply of the answer form on page 132. Place copies in the left-hand pocket of the folder.

Using the Center

1. The student reads each sentence and decides if it states a fact or an opinion.

2. Then the student writes the number of the sentence in the correct box on the answer form.

Name _____

Read each sentence. Decide if it states a fact or an opinion. Write the sentence number in the correct box.

Fact or Opinion?

Answer Form

Fact	Opinion

Bonus: Write a fact and an opinion about the following topics:

peanut butter

fact: _____

opinion: _____

homework

fact: _____

opinion: _____

Fact or Opinion?

Fact or Opinion?

A **fact** is something that is true. It is something that can be observed or measured.

An **opinion** is a personal view or belief. It cannot be said with complete certainty.

Follow these steps:

1. Take a sentence card and read it.

2. Decide if the sentence is a fact or an opinion.

3. Write the sentence number in the correct box on the answer form.

4. Repeat steps 1–3 with each sentence card.

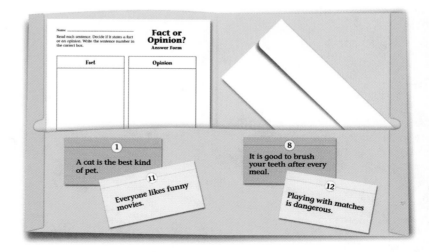

1

A cat is the best kind of pet.

2

Some dogs can be trained to do work.

3

It is wrong to take other people's property without asking.

4

Spinach is the best vegetable to eat if you want to have a strong body.

5

It is usually colder in the winter than in the spring.

6

Hamburgers taste better than hot dogs.

7

It is better to take a bath before you go to bed than in the morning.

8

It is good to brush your teeth after every meal.

9

$5.00 a week is the correct allowance for a third-grader.

10

Exercise can help you stay healthy.

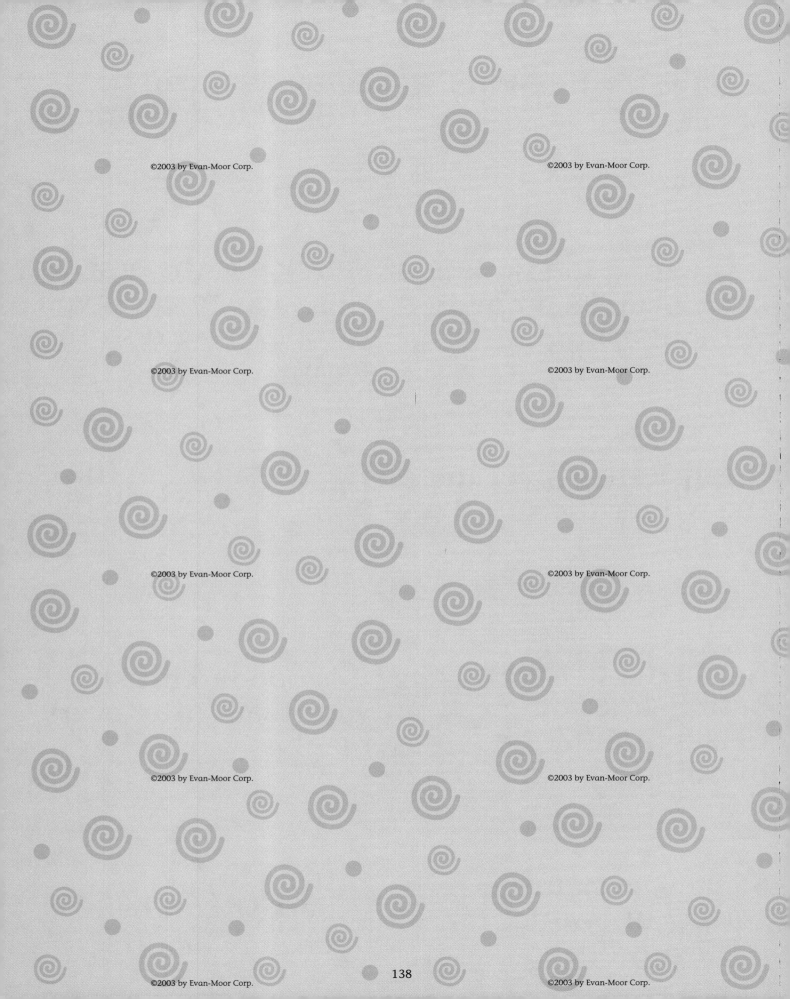

11

Everyone likes funny movies.

12

Playing with matches is dangerous.

13

A quarter is worth more than a dime.

14

Liver tastes terrible.

15

You should never walk in the rain.

16

The president of the United States has an office in the White House.

17

Some spiders are dangerous.

18

All birds have feathers.

19

It is more important to be good at sports than at art.

20

Butterflies are more beautiful than flowers.

Parts of Speech

How many sheep are in the pen?

Birds, squirrels, and lizards live in the trees in our backyard.

Snowflakes danced across the sky as the wind blew.

Preparing the Center

1. Prepare a folder following the directions on page 3. Laminate the cover design on page 143. Attach it to the front of the folder.

2. Laminate the student directions on page 145. Attach it to the back of the folder.

3. Laminate and cut out the task cards on pages 147, 149, 151, and 153. Place the cards from pages 147 and 149 in an envelope labeled *Parts of Speech—Set 1* and the cards from pages 151 and 153 in an envelope labeled *Parts of Speech—Set 2*. Place the envelopes in the right-hand pocket of the folder.

4. Reproduce a supply of the answer form on page 142. Place copies in the left-hand pocket of the folder.

Using the Center

1. The student takes one envelope and writes the set number on the answer form. Then the student selects a task card and decides what part of speech is represented by the word in color.

2. Finally, the student writes the word on the answer form in the appropriate box.

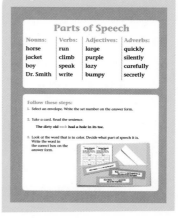

Name _____

Parts of Speech
Answer Form

Read each sentence. What part of speech do the word or words in color show? Write the word or words under the correct heading.

Set _____

Nouns
_____ _____
_____ _____

Verbs
_____ _____
_____ _____

Adjectives
_____ _____
_____ _____

Adverbs
_____ _____
_____ _____

Bonus: On the back of this form, write three sentences about your favorite animal. Circle these words in color:

nouns—red
verbs—blue
adjectives—green
adverbs—purple

Name _____

Parts of Speech
Answer Form

Read each sentence. What part of speech do the word or words in color show? Write the word or words under the correct heading.

Set _____

Nouns
_____ _____
_____ _____

Verbs
_____ _____
_____ _____

Adjectives
_____ _____
_____ _____

Adverbs
_____ _____
_____ _____

Bonus: On the back of this form, write three sentences about your favorite animal. Circle these words in color:

nouns—red
verbs—blue
adjectives—green
adverbs—purple

Literacy Centers—Take It to Your Seat • EMC 2124

Parts of Speech

Nouns:	Verbs:	Adjectives:	Adverbs:
horse	run	large	quickly
jacket	climb	purple	silently
boy	speak	lazy	carefully
Dr. Smith	write	bumpy	secretly

Follow these steps:

1. Select an envelope. Write the set number on the answer form.

2. Take a card. Read the sentence.

   The dirty old sock **had a hole in its toe.**

3. Look at the word that is in color. Decide what part of speech it is. Write the word in the correct box on the answer form.

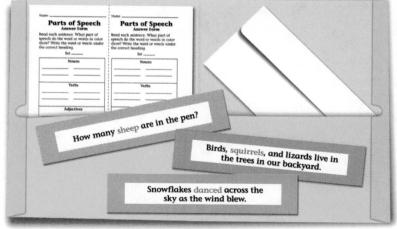

How many sheep are in the pen?

The horse ran across
the grassy field.

Lake Tahoe is in California.

The busy highway was filled
with speeding cars.

She walked slowly into the
dark room.

Please drive carefully.

set

1

set

1

set

1

set

1

set

1

set

1

Snowflakes danced across the sky as the wind blew.

A tired old man rested on the park bench.

The artist finally finished her painting for the show.

Anney chased her frisky pup down the street.

Father sang quietly to the fussy baby.

He completed his homework and then played a video game before dinner.

set
1

set
1

set
1

set
1

set
1

set
1

Birds, squirrels, and lizards live in the trees in our backyard.

Bats sleep hanging upside down in dark caves.

Mr. Brown always goes fishing on the weekend.

After hitting the ball with all his might, Stan raced around the bases.

The noontime sun shone brightly overhead.

After working on the car, Father soaked in a hot tub.

set

2

set

2

set

2

set

2

set

2

set

2

She laid her head on the soft pillow and quickly fell asleep.

The fish in the aquarium are hungry.

Carl won a shiny new skateboard in the contest.

The cold ice skaters drank the delicious hot chocolate.

Marcus played baseball yesterday.

The moon shone brightly in the dark night sky.

set
2

©2003 by Evan-Moor Corp.

set
2

©2003 by Evan-Moor Corp.

set
2

©2003 by Evan-Moor Corp.

set
2

©2003 by Evan-Moor Corp.

set
2

©2003 by Evan-Moor Corp.

set
2

©2003 by Evan-Moor Corp.

Table of Contents

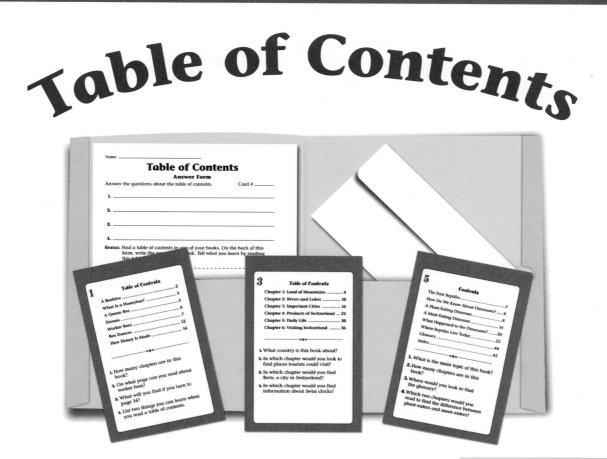

Preparing the Center

1. Prepare a folder following the directions on page 3. Laminate the cover design on page 157. Attach it to the front of the folder.

2. Laminate the student directions on page 159. Attach it to the back of the folder.

3. Laminate and cut out the task cards on pages 161, 163, and 165. Place the cards in an envelope. Label the envelope *Table of Contents*. Place the envelope in the right-hand pocket of the folder.

4. Reproduce a supply of the answer form on page 156. Place copies in the left-hand pocket of the folder.

Using the Center

1. The student selects a table of contents card and writes the card number on the answer form.

2. Then the student reads the card and answers the questions about the table of contents.

Name _____

Table of Contents
Answer Form

Answer the questions about the table of contents.   Card # _____

1. _____

2. _____

3. _____

4. _____

Bonus: Find a table of contents in one of your books. On the back of this form, write the name of the book. Tell what you learn by reading this table of contents.

- -

Name _____

Table of Contents
Answer Form

Answer the questions about the table of contents.   Card # _____

1. _____

2. _____

3. _____

4. _____

Bonus: Find a table of contents in one of your books. On the back of this form, write the name of the book. Tell what you learn by reading this table of contents.

Table of Contents

Your

Plants

Table of Contents

A table of contents shows what is in a book. It tells the number of the beginning page of each chapter.

Follow these steps:

1. Choose one Table of Contents card. Write the card number on the answer form.

2. Read the Table of Contents.

3. Write the answers to the questions on the answer form.

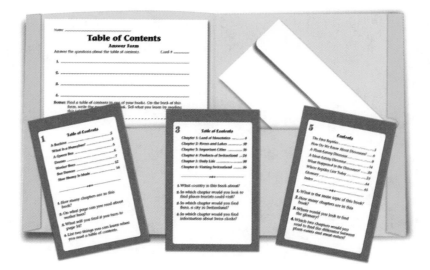

160

1

Table of Contents

● ● ●

1. How many chapters are in this book?

2. On what page can you read about worker bees?

3. What will you find if you turn to page 14?

4. List two things you can learn when you read a table of contents.

2

Table of Contents

● ● ●

1. What type of song is "Skip to My Lou"?

2. On what page will you find a picture to use for storytelling?

3. On what page will you find a Mother Goose rhyme?

4. Who is the author of "Rain"?

3

Table of Contents

1. What country is this book about?

2. In which chapter would you look to find places tourists could visit?

3. In which chapter would you find Bern, a city in Switzerland?

4. In which chapter would you find information about Swiss clocks?

4

Contents

1. What is the topic of this book?

2. Where would you find out how to check in for your flight?

3. Where would you read about what happens once the plane is in the air?

4. Where would you look to find the glossary and the index?

Contents

• • •

1. What is the main topic of this book?

2. How many chapters are in this book?

3. Where would you look to find the glossary?

4. Which two chapters would you read to find the difference between plant-eaters and meat-eaters?

This is a table of contents for a magazine.

MARCH 1996
VOLUME 8 NUMBER 3

• • •

1. What would you find on page 25 of this magazine?

2. What is the title of the poem?

3. On what page would you read about Jacques Cousteau?

4. Where would you send a letter to the magazine?

Using an Index

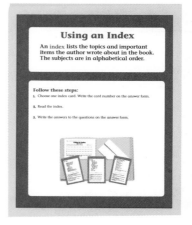

Preparing the Center

1. Prepare a folder following the directions on page 3. Laminate the cover design on page 169. Attach it to the front of the folder.

2. Laminate the student directions on page 171. Attach it to the back of the folder.

3. Laminate and cut out the task cards on pages 173, 175, and 177. Place the cards in an envelope. Label the envelope *Using an Index*. Place the envelope in the right-hand pocket of the folder.

4. Reproduce a supply of the answer form on page 168. Place copies in the left-hand pocket of the folder.

Using the Center

1. The student selects an index card and writes the card number on the answer form.

2. Then the student reads the card and answers the questions using the information in the index.

Name _____

Using an Index
Answer Form

Answer the questions using the index on the card.   Card # _____

1. _____

2. _____

3. _____

4. _____

Bonus: Find an index in one of your books. Write the name of the book. Tell how many topics are listed in the index.

- -

Name _____

Using an Index
Answer Form

Answer the questions using the index on the card.   Card # _____

1. _____

2. _____

3. _____

4. _____

Bonus: Find an index in one of your books. Write the name of the book. Tell how many topics are listed in the index.

Using an Index

Using an Index

An index lists the topics and important items the author wrote about in the book. The subjects are in alphabetical order.

Follow these steps:

1. Choose one index card. Write the card number on the answer form.

2. Read the index.

3. Write the answers to the questions on the answer form.

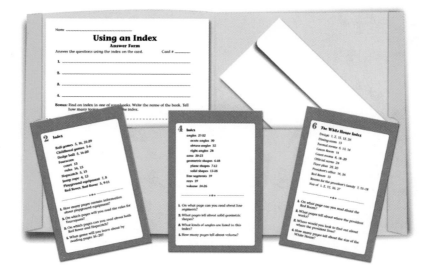

Literacy Centers—Take It to Your Seat • EMC 2124

1 About Reptiles Index

• • •

1. How many pages contain information about turtles?

2. On which pages will you read about eggs?

3. On which pages can you read about both alligators and crocodiles?

4. How are the topics arranged in an index?

---

2 Index

• • •

1. How many pages contain information about playground equipment?

2. On which pages will you read the rules for Foursquare?

3. On which pages can you read about both Red Rover and Hopscotch?

4. What game will you learn about by reading pages 16–20?

4 Index

1. On what page can you read about line segments?

2. What pages tell about solid geometric shapes?

3. What kinds of angles are listed in this index?

4. How many pages tell about volume?

---

3 Index

1. How many pages contain information about orb weavers?

2. On which pages can you read about tarantulas?

3. On which pages can you read about the parts of a spider?

4. Bolded numbers identify pages with pictures. On which pages will you find pictures of spiders?

6 The White House Index

● ●

1. On what page can you you read about the Red Room?

2. What pages tell about where the president works?

3. Where would you look to find out about where the president lives?

4. How many pages tell about the size of the White House?

---

5 Index

● ●

1. What type of book did this index come from?

2. List the four types of color you can learn about using this index.

3. Where would you probably find a list of art materials?

4. On what page can you read about how to mix watercolors?

Write a Story

Preparing the Center

1. Prepare a folder following the directions on page 3. Laminate the cover design on page 181. Attach it to the front of the folder.

2. Laminate the student directions on page 183. Attach it to the back of the folder.

3. Laminate and cut out the task cards on pages 185 and 187. Place the cards in an envelope. Label the envelope *Write a Story.* Place the envelope in the right-hand pocket of the folder.

4. Reproduce a supply of the answer form on page 180. Place copies in the left-hand pocket of the folder.

Using the Center

1. The student selects a story starter card.

2. Then the student writes a story.

Name _____

Write a Story
Answer Form

_____
title

_____

_____

_____

_____

_____

_____

_____

_____

_____

_____

_____

_____

Bonus: Illustrate your story on the back of this page.

Write a Story

Literacy Centers—Take It to Your Seat • EMC 2124

Write a Story

A story is an imaginative tale with a plot, characters, and a setting.

Follow these steps:

1. Choose a story starter card.

2. Plan your story.
   - Who is the story about?
   - What will happen in the story?
   - How will the story end?

3. Write your story. Use as many sheets of paper as you need.

4. Give your story a title.

As I was walking by the cornfield, I heard a strange voice calling my name.

The farmer's wife looked like a kindly old lady, but you can't always judge a book by its cover.

Mother Hen has just settled her chicks down for the night. Their fluffy little heads have begun to nod. It is time for a bedtime story.

What would it be like to be an egg hatching in the nest?

The rooster was sick and tired of getting up before dawn to crow the sun up. He packed his suitcase and headed off for a vacation.

Hector and Edgar discovered an old cobweb-covered trunk hidden in a corner of the barn. They cautiously lifted the lid.

Imagine you are the last pumpkin in the pumpkin patch.

The farmer's truck is stuck in a huge mud puddle. How is he going to get it out?

Answer Key

Page 5—Analogies

Set 1
thirsty : drink :: hungry : eat
happy : laugh :: sad : cry
eat : ate :: sleep : slept
finger : hand :: toe : foot
clock : tick :: bell: ring
room : house :: branch: tree
rooster : crow :: dog : bark
bear : den :: bee : hive
bird : sky :: fish : sea
car : garage :: stove : kitchen
peas : vegetable :: peach : fruit
ear : hear :: nose : smell

Set 2
computer : office :: tractor : farm
paint : artist :: guitar : musician
car : driver :: plane : pilot
woman : aunt :: man : uncle
speedy : pokey :: heavy : light
puppy : dog :: cub : bear
date : calendar :: time : clock
paw : bear :: fin : fish
scales : snake :: feathers : bird
hand : wrist :: foot : ankle
glass : break :: paper : tear
shoes : feet :: gloves : hands

Page 17—Multiple-Meaning Words
1. bat
2. pen
3. batter
4. fly
5. can
6. note
7. well
8. yard
9. trip
10. stick
11. bark
12. light

Page 31—Prefixes
disappear
disagree
dishonest
microwave
microscope
microphone
misbehave
misfortune
mistake
telephone
telescope
television
rewrite
reappear
redo
uncomfortable
unhappy
unable

Page 41—Suffixes
peaceful
graceful
thoughtful
kindness
sadness
darkness
teacher
painter
dancer
smartest
softest
quickest
comfortable
perishable
enjoyable
strengthen
frighten
lengthen

Page 51—Main Idea & Supporting Details

1 - **Main Idea**—Brownie is a smart dog.
Supporting Details:
  1. He can catch a Frisbee.
  2. He fetches the newspaper and carries it to Father.
  3. He can turn a backward flip on command.

2 - **Main Idea**—Seeds travel in many ways.
Supporting Details:
  1. Some seeds move in the wind.
  2. Some catch on fur of animals.
  3. People move seeds when they plant them.

3 - **Main Idea**—There are things to learn before you begin to snorkel.
Supporting Details:
  1. You need to learn how to breathe with a snorkel.
  2. You need to learn how to dive and swim wearing a mask and fins.
  3. You need to learn safety tips.

4 - **Main Idea**—Karla's brother is a pest.
Supporting Details:
  1. He knocked over her science project.
  2. He let her hamster out of its cage.
  3. He knocked grape juice into her lap.

5 - **Main Idea**—Jessie's room is very messy.
Supporting Details:
  1. Clothes and toys cover everything in the room.
  2. Pet hair and moldy food are on the floor and under the bed.
  3. The bed is unmade.

6 - **Main Idea**—A centipede is a great hunter.
Supporting Details:
  1. It stalks its prey.
  2. It poisons its prey.
  3. It catches silverfish, cockroaches, worms, and slugs.

Page 61—Antonyms

Set 1
  dawn—sunset
  answer—question
  follow—lead
  greedy—generous
  innocent—guilty
  liquid—solid

Set 2
  create—destroy
  problem—solution
  vanish—appear
  loose—tight
  timid—bold
  unique—common

Page 71—Synonyms

Set 1
  story—tale
  grab—seize
  build—construct
  mistake—error
  mend—repair
  use—operate

Set 2
  answer—reply
  locate—discover
  divide—separate
  eat—consume
  grateful—thankful
  freedom—liberty

Page 81—Combining Sentences

Sentences may be combined correctly in several different ways.

Page 95—Alphabetical Order

Set 1
1. camel
2. city
3. cookie
4. gauze
5. glance
6. ground
7. peculiar
8. phone
9. pickle
10. thunder
11. tiny
12. trailer

Set 2
1. faint
2. family
3. fantasy
4. fast
5. money
6. monster
7. motel
8. mouse
9. racket
10. raisin
11. rake
12. rattle

Set 3
1. bargain
2. barge
3. bark
4. barn
5. grace
6. grammar
7. grape
8. graph
9. weapon
10. wear
11. weather
12. weave

Page 107—Writing Descriptive Paragraphs
Students' writings will vary.

Page 121—Similes
Students' answers will vary.

Page 131—Fact or Opinion?
fact—2, 3, 5, 8, 10, 12, 13, 16, 17, 18

opinion—1, 4, 6, 7, 9, 11, 14, 15, 19, 20

Page 141—Parts of Speech

Set 1
Nouns—sheep, Lake Tahoe, homework
Verbs—ran, danced, finished
Adjectives—speeding, tired, frisky
Adverbs—slowly, carefully, quietly

Set 2
Nouns—squirrels, sun, aquarium
Verbs—sleep, raced, soaked, won
Adjectives—soft, delicious
Adverbs—always, yesterday, brightly

Page 155—Table of Contents

Card 1
1. There are seven chapters.
2. You will find out about worker bees on page 7.
3. You will read about how honey is made.
4. You can learn about what is in each chapter and the pages on which each chapter begins.

Card 2
1. It is an American folk song.
2. It is on page 12.
3. "One Misty, Moisty Morning" is on page 10.
4. The author of "Rain" is Garth Henry.

Card 3
1. It is about Switzerland.
2. You would look in chapter 6.
3. You would look in chapter 3.
4. You would look in chapter 4.

Card 4
1. This book is about taking a trip in an airplane.
2. You would read the chapter starting on page 12.
3. You would read the chapter starting on page 22.
4. The glossary begins on page 30. The index begins on page 34.

Card 5
1. This book is about dinosaurs.
2. There are six chapters in the book.
3. The glossary begins on page 44.
4. You would read the chapters beginning on pages 8 and 14 (or chapters 3 and 4).

Card 6
1. You would find out about a super contest you could enter.
2. The title of the poem is "Swim with the Dolphins."
3. You would begin reading on page 8.
4. You would send a letter to Readers' Mailbox.

Page 167—Using an Index

Card 1
1. Two pages are about turtles.
2. You read about eggs on pages 3, 9, 10, 27, 30, and 36.
3. You can read about both crocodiles and alligators on pages 3 and 4.
4. The topics are in alphabetical order.

Card 2
1. Two pages contain information about playground equipment.
2. The rules for Foursquare are on pages 14 and 15.
3. You can read about both Red Rover and Hopscotch on page 5.
4. You will learn about Dodge ball.

Card 3
1. Four pages contain information about orb weavers.
2. You can read about tarantulas on pages 19 through 22.
3. You can read about the parts of a spider on pages 9, 12, 14, and 28.
4. There are pictures of spiders on pages 11, 12, 18, 22, and 23.

Card 4
1. You can read about line segments on page 19.
2. You can read about solid shapes on pages 13 through 18.
3. Acute, obtuse, and right angles are listed in the index.
4. Three pages tell about volume.

Card 5
1. This index came from a book about art.
2. Complementary, cool, warm, and primary colors are listed in the index.
3. You would probably find a list of art materials on page 4 or 5.
4. You can read about mixing watercolors on page 53.

Card 6
1. You could read about the Red Room on page 13.
2. Pages 14 and 26 tell about the President's office (or where he works).
3. You would look at pages 7 and 15 through 18.
4. Five pages tell about the size of the White House.

Page 179—Write a Story
Students' writings will vary.